COLIN POWELL

Gloria D. Miklowitz

🎵 **Dominie Press, Inc.**

Publisher: Raymond Yuen
Editor: Bob Rowland
Designer: Greg DiGenti
Photo Credits: Reuters/Corbis (cover); Corbis (Page 11); U.S. Department of Defense/Helene Stikkel (Page 16); Peter Turnley/Corbis (Page 23); David Butow/Corbis (Page 24); and UPI (Page 27)

Text copyright © 2005 Gloria D. Miklowitz

All rights reserved. No part of this publication may be reproduced or transmitted in any form or by any means without permission in writing from the publisher. Reproduction of any part of this book, through photocopy, recording, or any electronic or mechanical retrieval system, without the written permission of the publisher, is an infringement of the copyright law.

Published by:

Dominie Press, Inc.

1949 Kellogg Avenue
Carlsbad, California 92008 USA

www.dominie.com

Paperback ISBN 0-7685-3043-1
Library Bound Edition ISBN 0-7685-3570-0
Printed in Singapore by PH Productions Pte Ltd
1 2 3 4 5 PH 07 06 05

Table of Contents

Chapter 1
Modest Beginnings...............................5

Chapter 2
**Distinguished
Military Graduate**...............................10

Chapter 3
Wounded in Action............................15

Chapter 4
An American Journey........................20

Chapter 5
A Life of Purpose...............................28

Glossary 31

Chapter 1

Modest Beginnings

The son of poor immigrant parents, Colin Powell grew up in the South Bronx in New York City and played stickball on the street with neighborhood friends. He wasn't a gifted athlete or a straight *A* student. Later, he scrubbed floors in a bottling plant to earn money for college. But from those modest beginnings, Colin Luther Powell distinguished himself as the first black officer to hold the nation's highest military post—chairman of the Joint Chiefs of Staff—and the first African American in U.S. history to become secretary of state.

Colin was born on April 5, 1937 in New York City. His parents were from the island of Jamaica in the West Indies. Luther, his father, came from a poor, farming family and had little education. He found work as a gardener, as an apartment house manager, and then finally in the New York garment industry, becoming foreman of a shipping department. Colin's parents met at a picnic. His mother, Maud Ariel (called Arie), was a high school graduate and was working as a seamstress. His parents married in 1929. Marilyn, their first child, was born in 1931.

When Colin was about six, his family moved from Harlem to the South Bronx. It was a lower middle-class neighborhood of many different ethnic groups. Every few blocks a person could stop in at a Jewish bakery, a Puerto Rican grocery store, or an Italian shoe repair shop. Colin once said that he enjoyed growing up there because so many aunts, uncles, and cousins were nearby.

From his earliest years Colin played street games with his neighborhood friends, but he was not much of an athlete, nor was he a very good student. His sister, Marilyn, was an excellent student, so Colin's grades were a disappointment to the Powells, who valued education and saw it as the best way to escape poverty.

Colin took piano and then flute lessons, but had no talent for either. It seemed he was no musician, no athlete, and no student. He was only a happy boy with many good friends.

In 1950 Colin entered Morris High School in the South Bronx. "I was still directionless, not fired by anything," he said. "My pleasure was hanging out with the guys, making the walk from Kelly Street to Westchester Avenue and back, going to movies on Saturday mornings and church on Sundays." He never smoked marijuana or used other drugs. "My father would have killed me," he said.

During those years Colin worked at Sicksers, a Jewish children's furniture and toy store. The owner liked him because he was always on time. Colin worked hard and learned to speak some Yiddish, a language that is spoken by about 4 million Jewish people all over the world. Soon the owner had Colin selling furniture as well as unpacking boxes, but he also encouraged him to get an education and not count on the store for his future income.

Colin graduated from high school in 1953 with a *C+* grade average and applied for college at New York University (NYU) and the City College of New York (CCNY). Both schools accepted him, but NYU cost $750 a year and CCNY cost just $10. The decision was driven by the family's limited finances. Colin went to CCNY.

Chapter 2

Distinguished Military Graduate

To earn money for schoolbooks and clothes, Colin worked as a porter and washed floors at a bottling plant, where he earned $65 a week. "Whatever skill the job required, I mastered," he said. "All work is honorable."

Colin Powell with his wife, Alma, and their three children, Linda, Anne, and Michael

"Education meant the difference between wrapping packages or sewing buttons all day and having a real profession," Colin wrote in his best-selling book, *My American Journey: An Autobiography*.

In the 1950s, some of the best jobs in America were in engineering. Earning enough to support a family meant a lot to the Powells. "That's where the money is,"

Colin's mother advised, so he chose engineering as his major at CCNY. The first course he took was mechanical drawing. One day the instructor told the class to draw "a cone intersecting a plane in space." Colin just sat there, unable to visualize the drawing. "If this was engineering, the game was over," he said.

At that point, Colin decided to switch his major to geology. His security-minded parents wondered what kind of a job he could get as a geologist, and if that job would come with a pension, or income after retirement.

While college classes didn't excite Colin, the Reserve Officer's Training Corps (ROTC) on campus did. CCNY had the biggest voluntary ROTC in America at the time, with 1,500 cadets at the height of the Korean War. Colin said he liked the uniform as well as "the discipline, the structure, the camaraderie, the sense of belonging." He became a leader almost immediately in the Pershing Rifles, a division of ROTC.

The 1950s saw the birth of the Civil Rights Movement in America. Rosa Parks, Martin Luther King, and other names would become familiar to most Americans as the fight for equality gained momentum. But the struggle was far from over. Colin had his first experience with blatant prejudice during summer training at Fort Bragg, in North Carolina, when he was denied service at a restaurant. As in other places in the South, black people there had to use separate restrooms and water fountains. They couldn't sit at lunch counters with white people.

Race, color, background, and income weren't as important in the military as they were in the larger society. Soldiers who fought together would go the limit for each other and the group. If this was what soldiering was about, Colin wanted it.

Colin graduated from CCNY in June 1958 with a bachelor's degree in geology and a *C* average. But he excelled in ROTC and was named a "distinguished military graduate." Many young men his age were being drafted into the Army for a two-year tour of duty. Instead of waiting to be drafted, Colin joined the Army and was commissioned a second lieutenant. He was sent to Germany in October 1958. Two years later he was assigned to Fort Devens in Massachusetts, near Boston. There, he met Alma Johnson, a young woman who came from a family of educators and business people. Alma was impressed by Colin's warmth, intelligence, and drive.

Chapter 3

Wounded in Action

Colin married Alma Johnson in August 1962, two years after they first met. One month after their wedding, he was transferred to Fort Bragg, North Carolina. At the end of a six-week training session on firearms, he was

Former Secretary of Defense Dick Cheney administers the oath of office to Colin Powell, chairman of the Joint Chiefs of Staff, as Powell's wife, Alma, looks on

named second-best cadet in the entire camp. "You know why you weren't named first?" a supply sergeant asked him. "You think these ROTC instructors are going to go back to their colleges and say the best kid was a Negro?"

"I did not feel inferior, and I was not going to let anybody make me believe I was," Colin said. He saw the Army as a profession that would let him go as far as his talents would take him. After three years' service Colin could have left the Army in 1961, "But I did not know anything but soldiering," he said.

Alma returned to her parents' home in Birmingham, Alabama when Colin was assigned to Vietnam in 1963. Their first child, Michael, was born while Colin was away. He kept a picture of his little son in his pocket while he fought in the jungles of Vietnam.

The war in Vietnam proved to be a divisive period in the United States. Public opinion was sharply divided over the war. Conditions on the battlefield were especially difficult and dangerous. One day, while leading a unit through a rice paddy, Colin stepped on a booby trap, a stick that pierced his left foot through his boot. He later received a Purple Heart for being wounded in action. That was to be one of many awards and service medals he would receive during his thirty-five year career in the military.

Colin completed two tours of duty in Vietnam. One day, while he was on an inspection trip in a helicopter, the pilot tried to land in a small jungle clearing. The copter crashed. Colin leaped from the smoking wreckage, knowing the chopper could explode. He ran back to the smoldering helicopter and managed to rescue several soldiers before it exploded in a ball of flames. For his heroism, he was awarded the Soldiers' Medal.

Between 1970 and 1971, Colin was back in the United States and living with his wife, Alma, and their three children, Michael, Linda, and Anne.

He worked at the Pentagon and took classes for a master's degree in business administration. Only thirty-four years old, and with fifteen years in the military, Colin was becoming more and more valuable to the government and the military. His next move up was to win a White House fellowship.

The fellowship was "a dream job," he later said. It put him in touch with important people who got to know and respect him. When the fellowship ended, he returned to Army life as a battalion commander in South Korea. There, he was responsible for the lives of nearly 5,000 men and women.

Next he was chosen to attend the National War College, in Washington, D.C.—one more step toward greater responsibility.

Chapter 4

An American Journey

Whenever a new president takes office, there are changes in who runs the government. Colin realized that. He decided that to be useful when these changes happened, he had to keep up with new developments in his field. In the next years he moved from one assignment to another, returning to school for more training when needed. Colin "did not spend time flattering people. He was a very, very strong and wise person who understood the complexities of government," a Defense Department official said.

When asked by Defense Secretary Casper Weinberger to leave the Army and go to work for him, Colin turned him down. He preferred being with troops over dealing with elected and government officials. After much discussion, Weinberger convinced him. President Ronald Reagan needed a strong and wise military adviser, and Colin "fit the bill."

In accepting Weinberger's offer, Colin became the messenger between the White House and the Defense

Department for three years. He acted as Weinberger's eyes and ears, talking on the phone and face-to-face with politicians, picking up bits of information he thought his boss needed. He worked hard, often at his desk by 6:30 in the morning until after 7 at night. In working at the Pentagon, it was possible for Colin to live at home and get to know his three growing children.

His assignments varied between the Pentagon in Washington, D. C. and the Army. In Leavenworth, Kansas, where he served for a time, Colin arranged for a memorial to be built to honor black soldiers. They were men who had fought for our country in every war. They proved themselves equal to white soldiers but were never treated equally. A Confederate general said of black soldiers that they should be used for

General Colin Powell during the Gulf War, 1991

digging and chopping, "But don't arm them. If slaves will make good soldiers, our whole theory of slavery is wrong."

For six months, Colin commanded the V Corps in Frankfurt, West Germany.

Colin Powell autographs copies of his book,
My American Journey: An Autobiography

It was an army of almost 100,000 troops. He later said that when commanding V Corps he was "probably the happiest general in the world."

Every assignment earned him praise for his organizational skills, good sense, and ability to get along with difficult people.

On his desk, he kept a list of some basic rules he tried to live by. They include:

- *Get mad. Then get over it.*
- *It can be done!*
- *Be careful what you choose. You may get it.*
- *Don't let adverse facts stand in the way of a good decision.*
- *You can't make someone else's choices. You shouldn't let someone else make yours.*
- *Share the credit.*
- *Remain calm.*
- *Be kind.*
- *Have a vision.*
- *Be demanding.*

These rules guided Colin through some difficult years when there were wars in many different parts of the world. His military knowledge and government experience proved invaluable.

Colin became the assistant to the president for national security affairs in 1987. He left that position in 1989 to become chairman of the Joint Chiefs of Staff, the highest military post in the country. He served as chairman from 1989 to 1993, under both President George H. W. Bush and President Bill Clinton.

In his work as head of the Joint Chiefs of Staff, Colin drew international attention and praise as one of the main planners of the 1991 Gulf War. In that conflict, the United States and its allies drove back an invasion by Iraq of one of its oil-rich neighbors, Kuwait.

In 1993, Colin, a four-star General and Chairman of the Joint Chiefs of Staff, decided that it was time to retire. He felt that the Army had been good to him. Among the mementoes he brought home were a bust of Thomas Jefferson and a framed plaque that read, "Lincoln freed the slaves, but Martin Luther King set the rest of the nation free."

Colin Powell is presented with the highest honor awarded by the National Association for the Advancement of Colored People at the NAACP's annual national convention in 1991

After his retirement, Colin began working on his book, *My American Journey: An Autobiography*. That move would prove to open yet another chapter in a lifetime already marked by great accomplishments.

Chapter 5

A Life of Purpose

In 1995, Colin went on a nationwide tour to promote his autobiography. As he traveled across the country, rumors spread that he would become a candidate in the 1996 presidential campaign. But on November 9, 1995, Colin held a news conference and announced to the nation that he would not enter the race.

During his military career, Colin received many awards and medals. In addition to the Purple Heart he was awarded in Vietnam, he won a Bronze Star, a Legion of Merit Award, a Distinguished Service Medal, and a Soldier's Medal.

Colin also has received a number of civilian honors. His awards include two Presidential Medals of Freedom. He has also been awarded a Congressional Gold Medal and an honorary knighthood from the queen of England. Several schools have been named after him. And he has honorary degrees from universities and colleges across the country.

In addition to his many military contributions to his country, Colin has devoted himself to various social causes. He has served on the board of trustees of the historically black Howard University, and the board of directors of the United Negro College Fund. Colin also was on the board of governors of the Boys and Girls Clubs of America and the advisory board of the Children's Health Fund, a nonprofit organization that provides medical care to poor and homeless children.

In 2001 President George W. Bush appointed Colin to be the Secretary of State. He was the first African American to hold that position.

Colin Powell's success stems from all he has given in service to America.

"I believe in the system we have in this country," he said. "I believe in the fundamental goodness of people. I believe in my family. I believe in myself. And I believe that God gave us life to use for a purpose."

Glossary

Adverse – difficult; unfavorable; unpleasant.

Autobiography – the story of a person's life, written by that person. (A *biography* is the story of a person's life written by someone else.)

Booby Trap – a concealed device used as a weapon that is designed to go off when someone touches it.

Bronze Star – a high U.S. military honor awarded to any member of the armed forces who performs a heroic act during combat.

Camaraderie – a spirit of strong friendship and mutual support.

Divisive – creating strong opposing feelings among people.

Drive – ambition; energy; determination.

Ethnic Groups – people who share a common racial or national background.

Geology – a science that studies the physical history of the Earth.

Germany – an industrialized country in Central Europe. (The capital of Germany is Berlin.)

Honorary Degrees – certificates of graduation given to people in recognition of their great accomplishments, even though they haven't completed the necessary coursework.

Invaluable – important beyond measure; priceless.

Iraq – a country in Southwest Asia. (The capital of Iraq is Baghdad.)

Kuwait – a country in Southwest Asia. (The capital of Kuwait is Kuwait City.)

Major – in college, a student's main area of study.

Mementoes – souvenirs; small things used to remind someone of a journey or an experience.

Modest – ordinary, humble, or down-to-earth.

Momentum – strength or force gained over time through a series of events.

News Conference – a gathering of reporters from the news media.

Pentagon – headquarters of the United States Department of Defense. It is one of the world's largest office buildings. (The Pentagon is a five-sided building. *Pentagon* comes from the Greek word *pente*, meaning *five*.)

Prejudice – the result of a disapproving opinion formed without just grounds.

Purple Heart – a high U.S. military honor awarded to any member of the armed forces who is wounded or killed in action.

Reserve Officer's Training Corps (ROTC) – a program that enables students to study and train for the military while they complete their college education.

Seamstress – a woman who sews and works with fabric for a living.

South Korea - a country in eastern Asia. (The capital of South Korea is Seoul.)

Stickball – a form of baseball played on the street using a broomstick instead of a bat.

Unit – a group of soldiers who are part of a military force.

Vietnam – a country in Southeast Asia. (The capital of Vietnam is Hanoi.)